SIXTY SECONDS TO SUCCESS

Change Your Life in a Minute with These Peak Performance Tips

Edward W. Smith

First Edition

Bright Moment, Englewood, New Jersey

SIXTY SECONDS TO SUCCESS
Change Your Life in a Minute with These Quick Peak
Performance Tips
by Edward W. Smith

Published by:
Bright Moment
Post Office Box 8106
Englewood, NJ 07631-8106 USA
Orders@brightmoment.com
http://brightmoment.com
201-568-0019

Unattributed quotations are by Edward W. Smith.

ISBN, print ed. 0-9754164-0-5

SAN   256-033X

First Printing 2004

Cover Design: Jo-Ann Do (vibecity2@yahoo.com)
Composition: Midatlantic Books and Journals, Inc.

Library of Congress Cataloging-in-Publication Data

Library of Congress Control Number: 2004094745

Smith, Edward W.
    Sixty seconds to success: change your life in a minute with these quick peak performance tips.
        S. cm.
ISBN 0-9754164-0-5
1. Sixty Seconds to Success-United States.   2. Self-help.

Table of Contents

About the Author

Edward Smith is the producer and host of the *Bright Moment* cable TV show. The show has a "success/peak performance" theme and features interviews with experts in fields related to peak performance. Prior to having the TV show, he had the *Bright Moment* radio show with a similar theme. He is the president of the Bright Moment^{SM} Seminars, which use a unique "interview with an expert" format to increase employee productivity. Edward Smith is also a motivational speaker, specializing in helping people find their true interests in life. He does voice-over work and acts in TV commercials. He lives in Englewood, NJ with his wife, Theresa, and his cat, Lily. Additional information is available on his Web site, brightmoment.com.

Dedication and Acknowledgements

This book is dedicated to my wife, Theresa Smith, and my sister Virginia Smith. Both have given me large amounts of encouragement, suggestions and help just when it was needed. I love both of them very much. Special mention goes to my cat, Lily, who throughout the writing of the book helped to keep me on an even keel and grounded in understanding of what life is all about.

In addition, I would like to acknowledge the motivational writers and speakers that have been an influence in my life and work:

Ed Agresta	Susan Race
Les Brown	Anthony Robbins
Bob Burg	Jim Rohn
Jack Canfield	Rich Ruffalo
Steven Covey	Brendan Tobin
Dr. Wayne Dyer	Brian Tracy
David Denotaris	Mike Tully
Jim Donovan	Dennis Waitley
Dr. Rob Gilbert	Zig Ziglar
Mark Victor Hansen	Dr. Suzanne Zoglio

I would like to thank Fred Ambrogio for developing the name for this book. I would also like to thank Jo-Ann Do, who created the book cover design, plus Anna Szabados of

Mission College, for her support of the design work. Special thanks go to Philip Goetz of TRBSolutions.com, who has been instrumental in making the Internet work for me, by combining his technical skills with people and business skills, and keeping the project moving on a timely basis. Also my editor, Alice Lawler, should be recognized for her great job in editing this book.

Advisory/Disclaimer

This book is designed to provide information on techniques for moving your life ahead. It is sold with the understanding that the publisher and author are not engaged in rendering medical, psychological or other professional advice. If a service such as these, or other expert assistance is required, the services of a competent professional should be sought at once.

It is not the purpose of this book to reprint all the information that is otherwise available to people looking for self-help information, but instead to complement, amplify and supplement other texts. You are urged to read all of the available self-help material, attend seminars, listen to tapes, etc., and tailor the information to your particular needs.

Success does not come easily, even with the advice given in this book. Action is required to attain the knowledge, and more action is required to implement it. This translates into work, and while the information in this book will increase your chances of success, it does not guarantee it.

Every effort has been made to make this book as complete and as accurate as possible. However, there may be mistakes, both typographical and in content. Therefore, this book should only be used as a general guide, and not as the ultimate source to improve your life.

Introduction

Sixty Seconds to Success is a collection of short, action-oriented tips on how you can run your life even better. Each page contains one tip, plus space for you to write notes on what actions you plan to take as a result of reading the tip. So each page provides you with something you can do, RIGHT NOW, to help you move towards your goals. These tips work, regardless of who you are, and where you are in the process of attaining the life you want. In addition, by writing the steps you plan to take as a result of a tip, you "etch" this tip into your mind and make a commitment to follow up on this new knowledge. This has the effect of giving you hope and improving your morale, along with your performance.

The tips in *Sixty Seconds to Success* are compiled from the "One Minute Motivators" that open the *Bright Moment* radio and TV show and the Bright Moment Seminars.

Sixty Seconds to Success can be used in several ways. It can be read for tips to jump-start your performance right now. It can also be used as a workbook to plot steps for you to take in order to prepare yourself for the next level. Regardless of how you use *Sixty Seconds to Success*, remember one thing. All of the knowledge in the book, or all the knowledge in the world for that matter, will not do you any good unless you TAKE ACTION. So pick a tip from the book right now and start taking the steps recommended there, and you will find that every moment in your life will be a Bright Moment.

Good luck.

CHAPTER 1

Know What You Want out of Life

Knowing what you want out of life is the single most important thing you can do. "Success is getting what you want; happiness is wanting what you get." Take time to be clear about what you want out of life. We are bombarded with ads for products to bring back our vitality, energy, etc. What you really need is to have a dream, and the energy will follow. One of the tragedies of life is that many of the people who actually make it to the top of their fields are miserable once they are there, because they never took the time to ask themselves what they really want out of life.

Few of us know what we want, other than the broad objectives, such as having lots of money, etc. Take the time to break these broad objectives into smaller objectives, so you get a better understanding of what you really want out of life, and make the goals more achievable. One way to do this is to follow your dreams. Your instincts are telling you that there is something you would be good at and enjoy. Listen to those voices telling you those things and follow your dream. You will discover talents you never knew you had, because you are not given an idea without the power to make it happen.

ACTION STEPS I WILL TAKE TO
FIND WHAT I WANT OUT OF LIFE

Ask yourself if you were starting out fresh today, would you choose the same job, company, business, school, etc., that you have right now. If the answer is "no," then why are you spending time trying to hold something together that you know is not right for you now? Your time is a fixed commodity, and if you are using it up, trying to hold off the inevitable, take your finger out of the dyke and run for it. Take the steps needed in order to get yourself into a new place. No one will come to your rescue; you must prepare yourself and take action, and all of this takes time. Give up on your losing situation and focus on what will work in the future, so you can start today to work on your new life.

ACTION STEPS I WILL TAKE TO
BUILD A LIFE THAT I WANT

_____

_____

_____

_____

_____

CHAPTER 2

Goals

You can change your future, if you change your goals. You are not stuck where you are now, forever. You can change your future, if you decide that you want something different. If you are not happy with where you are now, give careful thought to where you would like to be, and then start planning what it takes to get what you need to get there. Then, most importantly, start to implement the plan.

**ACTION STEPS I WILL TAKE TO
SET GOALS I WANT TO ATTAIN**

_____

_____

_____

_____

Here is something that definitely works: getting definite about your plans. If you lay out what you want to accomplish in specific terms, it has a greater chance of happening than if you just have some vague ideas floating around in your head. Take your vacation, for example. Chances are pretty good that you ended up when and where you wanted to be on vacation. Chances are also pretty good that you spent some time going over brochures, looking at costs, checking calendars, etc., to get most of the details worked out.

The rest of your life is no different. Any business or personal plans that you give the same amount of effort to will probably happen. Imagine, you can really have what you want; you just have to plan for it. It is true, if you focus on what you want and get specific about how you can make it happen, you will probably get it. So if you definitely want to accomplish something, get definite about it.

**ACTION STEPS I WILL TAKE TO
GET DEFINITE ABOUT MY PLANS**

_____

_____

_____

_____

_____

CHAPTER 3

Things to Do Every Day

Every day, ask yourself, "How can I be a better..."? Whatever you want to be better at should be reviewed every day. Remind yourself every day that you want to get better at something you are working on, and make it a point to think about it. This will bring gradual progress in key areas of your life, and after a period of time, you will be a true expert in something.

ACTION STEPS I WILL TAKE TO
IMPROVE IN SOME WAY TODAY

_____

_____

_____

_____

_____

Start and end the day with positive messages to yourself. Make your first thoughts of the day, as well as the last ones, positive. Read something positive, or write yourself positive notes to consider, just before going to bed and just after rising. You will sleep better and be in a better mood throughout the day as a result of this, and your productivity will be higher.

**ACTION STEPS I WILL TAKE TO
START/END THE DAY WELL**

_____

_____

_____

_____

_____

CHAPTER 4

Success

Become an overnight success. Ever notice how some people become overnight successes and wonder why you can't be as successful? Well, let me let you in on a secret. Most of those people who became an "overnight success" have worked for years, getting the education they need, the experience they need, making plans, focusing on their priorities and quietly going about their business. Then the day came when they were ready, they saw their chance, they took action and presto, they were OVERNIGHT SUCCESSES. So if you want to be an overnight success too, keep your nose to the grindstone, get ready, and when you see your opportunity, TAKE ACTION, and you will be an overnight success as well.

ACTION STEPS I WILL TAKE TO
BECOME AN OVERNIGHT SUCCESS

_____

_____

_____

_____

_____

Set up a small win, to make sure you have a big win. Nothing succeeds like success, as success builds you up to have more successes. You practice harder after a win than after a loss. Your self-confidence goes up after a win, so you try more things, and the more you try, the more you win. So to have bigger wins, you should set up small successes that will breed more successes.

**ACTION STEPS I WILL TAKE TO
SET UP A SMALL WIN RIGHT NOW**

_____

_____

_____

_____

_____

CHAPTER 5

Use Positive Self-Talk

Change "I don't know" to "I am going to find out." Many of us end a period of thinking about something with the phrase, "Oh I don't know." This causes us to stop working on the problem and creates a downward cycle in our results. We convince ourselves we don't know. If you change it to, "I am going to find out," your subconscious keeps working on the situation, and you have a positive view of it. Most of all you have hope.

"I am going to find out" should be your motto. You have the capacity to learn, so you are not tied down by any past defeat in your life. Wisdom always triumphs over adversity. Use "I am going to find out" whenever you are struggling to figure out why you had a problem. That way you will open yourself up to positive thoughts and put a positive spin on the situation, and you won't feel stuck. Plus you will learn what you need to learn in order to avoid the problem in the future and to be able to move ahead with your life.

ACTION STEPS I WILL TAKE TO SAY, "I AM GOING TO FIND OUT"

_____

_____

_____

_____

_____

Change the phrase, "if only" to, "next time." Instead of saying, "If only I was better prepared," say, "Next time I will be better prepared." "If only" focuses on past failures, whereas "next time" focuses on future successes and builds your resilience.

**ACTION STEPS I WILL TAKE TO
SAY, "NEXT TIME"**

_____

_____

_____

_____

CHAPTER 6

Work Harder

Increase your performance by 1 percent and you can be at the top of most fields. It doesn't sound like much, but look at the difference in the performance levels for the top athletes. The difference in time between first and second place for the top runners and bike racers is usually seconds for a race that took several hours. Even more amazing is the fact that this matter of seconds in that event comes after months and months, or sometimes years, of practice. Being 1 percent better than the others would have put the winners so far ahead, there wouldn't have been anyone else that came close.

This holds true for you as well. In almost every field, being 1 percent better than you are now would put you at the top of your field. Start to think of how you can make small improvements in your performance, as that may be all that is needed to take you to the top.

ACTION STEPS I WILL TAKE TO
IMPROVE MY PERFORMANCE BY 1 PERCENT

_____

_____

_____

_____

_____

If you are willing to do things that other people aren't willing to do, you will get things that other people won't get. If you are willing to prepare more than others do, plan more than others do, work out more than others do, etc., you will get rewards that other people won't get.

**ACTION STEPS I WILL TAKE TO
DO THINGS OTHER PEOPLE WON'T DO**

_____

_____

_____

_____

_____

CHAPTER 7

Decision Making

Make a decision and if it is the wrong decision, make another decision. Stop putting off making decisions until you have all the information you need, because you will never have all the information you need. Make the decision with the best information you have, but make the decision now. Your life will suddenly fall into line with the decision you made, and most of the time things will go better for you. If things don't go right, change and make a new decision.

You also can tie this into a pattern of learning to take more chances in your life. They don't have to be big risks, but you need to learn to take more chances if you want a different outcome in your life. Not everything will work out, but the fact that you are taking risks, even if small ones, will add excitement to your life and give you some payoffs in terms of getting what you want.

ACTION STEPS I WILL TAKE TO
MAKE DECISIONS NOW

_____

_____

_____

_____

_____

Create a board of directors for yourself. Create an imaginary group of advisors to help you make decisions. Make up a list of the top experts in the field you are making a decision in, and ask yourself what each of those people would probably tell you to do. Read their books, check their Web sites, etc., and get an insight into their thinking, then bring it back to your decision. You will be amazed by how just asking yourself how an expert you have in mind would handle it, will improve your decision making.

Imagine someone who has the answers to your problem, and imagine what they would say to you about your problem. Formulate your problem into a question worded in a way you think they would understand, write it down, and then sit or stand in a different place from where you were before. Pretend you are the "expert" and say or write what you think the "expert" would tell you.

ACTION STEPS I WILL TAKE TO
USE EXPERT ADVICE

_____

_____

_____

_____

CHAPTER 8

Take Action

Give your ideas wings. You have a number of great ideas every day, but most of us let them go by without taking any action. Take the next great idea you have, and start the steps needed to make it happen, as soon as you have the idea. Don't let the great ideas fade away without action. Use the momentum you have when you are excited about the idea, to propel you into implementing it.

You need to take action when an idea strikes you. Your emotional involvement is highest at that point and it can help propel you into action. If you wait, your urgency starts to diminish, and your great idea is lost. So start to act on your big idea as soon as it hits you and you will find you accomplish a lot more quality things.

**ACTION STEPS I WILL TAKE TO
IMPLEMENT MY IDEAS NOW**

_____

_____

_____

_____

Strive for excellence, not perfection. Don't get it perfect—just get it going. We waste a lot of time trying to make something perfect and then end up not finishing it. Excellence is much more cost efficient than perfection. Spending that extra time and money to make something absolutely perfect is rarely worth it from a payback standpoint. It is easy to get caught up in a project, trying to make it perfect; however, we soon find our budget for time and funds is running out. If instead we aim to make our product or service "excellent," it still gives us a big advantage over most of the competition. We can use the time and money we would have spent to make it perfect to go on to another project that will move us ahead even faster. So if you want to increase your overall efficiency, strive for excellence, and not for perfection.

ACTION STEPS I WILL TAKE TO
STRIVE FOR EXCELLENCE, NOT PERFECTION

_____

_____

_____

_____

_____

CHAPTER 9

Discipline

Perseverance is not one long race; it is a series of short races, won, one after another. Many people think the "short races" or seemingly minor things do not count when it comes to perseverance, but in fact, this is what perseverance is all about. Your projects, your goals and your whole life are a series of short races, all linked to the direction you want to go. By neglecting the short races, you will never accumulate the "wins" you need to attain your goal.

**ACTION STEPS I WILL TAKE TO
WIN THE SHORT RACES**

_____

_____

_____

_____

_____

Looking for some quick tips on how to run your life? Follow the Ten Commandments, regardless of your religious beliefs. The Ten Commandments offer solid advice on how to run your life in an efficient manner and will keep you from falling prey to many of the things that knock us off course in the pursuit of our goals. Study the Ten Commandments, put them into action, and watch your life come together. Follow the Ten Commandments and your life and the whole world will work better.

You don't have to be religious to follow most of the commandments; they are just good advice for you and the world in general. Think of how many problems you have right now, that you wouldn't have, if you had truly followed the Ten Commandments. Review them and take them out of a religious context and see how relevant they are to the problems and decisions you are facing every day.

**ACTION STEPS I WILL TAKE TO
USE THE TEN COMMANDMENTS AS A GUIDE**

_____

_____

_____

_____

_____

CHAPTER 10

Ask for Help

Ask for help. Asking for help is not a sign that you are not good enough—it is a signal that you want to do and be your best. Don't try to reinvent the wheel, unless you need to learn from it. Ask for help in any area you need it, be it physical, mental, or even spiritual. We can't do everything as well as someone else, and it is a waste of time and effort to try to do something that another person can do for you faster and easier.

Use the help you are given to move your life ahead and be the best you can be. But be careful to ask the right people for help. When we need help, all too often we ask whomever is convenient, rather than the person best suited to give us the help we need. Asking the wrong person for advice can create more problems than it solves. Make sure you know that the person you ask has had good experiences with what you are asking and really knows the information you are seeking. Be selective in whom you ask for help.

**ACTION STEPS I WILL TAKE TO
ASK THE RIGHT PEOPLE FOR HELP**

_____

_____

_____

_____

_____

You need a coach. No one makes it in the world of sports without a coach. Just because you aren't a professional athlete doesn't mean you don't need a coach. You need a coach in your business and personal life as much as an Olympic athlete needs one. You are good at many things, but you can be better at all of them. Having someone to teach you shortcuts, and better methods, can move your business or personal life to the next level. I use the word coach, but they can also be referred to as a mentor, an expert, or a consultant.

Think of how much time you have spent struggling with a problem and then found someone who solved it right away. Think of how much better you would be if many of the issues you were struggling with could be cleared up just as fast. So think of the issues you are working on, and then start to think of who can help you. Help is out there if you look for it, and your business and personal life will move to the fast track once you find it.

ACTION STEPS I WILL TAKE TO
GET A COACH

_____

_____

_____

_____

_____

CHAPTER 11

Change Something That
Is Not Working

Here are two great reasons to do something. Number one is that you have never done it that way before, and number two is that you tried it before and it didn't work. As you know, those are also the most common reasons for NOT doing something and they have killed more new ideas than anything else has. Why not reverse the logic on these two common objections to doing something and see what happens?

Trying something that *hasn't* been tried before might be just what is needed to move your project ahead. Trying something that *has* been tried before might work because things are different now. When you are having a problem, you need to be creative in your approach to solving it, and so I urge you not to shut your thinking off by using the above objections. Instead tell yourself to try something new or to relook at something that was tried before. If you do that, you will be surprised at what great new approaches you will come up with.

**ACTION STEPS I WILL TAKE TO
APPROACH THINGS DIFFERENTLY**

_____

_____

_____

_____

_____

You need a change of pace. When you want things to go better, you are feeling stuck, etc., you need to shake things up. Drive home a different way, eat someplace different for lunch, go into a store you normally wouldn't go into. Every time you are exposed to something different, even if it is something that seems small and insignificant, you are forced to look at things differently.

When you look at things differently, you still bring your old concerns with you, so those old concerns get looked at with this new information. And from that you can get some very creative insights into things that have been bogging you down. So start right now, and begin to change little things you do out of habit and then go back to some of the things that were bogging you down. I will bet a new approach will come to you.

ACTION STEPS I WILL TAKE TO
DO THINGS DIFFERENTLY

_____

_____

_____

_____

_____

CHAPTER 12

Role Models and the People You Associate With

Looking for a role model to follow? Be the person your friends say you are, and avoid being the person your enemies say you are. Follow the positive traits people say you have and build on them. You will find people drawn to you and they will help you succeed.

ACTION STEPS I WILL TAKE TO
BE THE BEST PERSON I CAN BE

_____

_____

_____

_____

_____

For one hour today, step into the role of the person you want to be. Be that person totally. Talk like they would, walk like they would, read what they would read, even eat what they would eat. Do whatever it takes to get into the role completely. Notice how you feel, how you approach decisions, what you do and what you don't do. At the end of the hour, ask yourself what part of that role you can take on right now and keep going. Tomorrow do it again, and sooner or later, you will become the person you want to be.

ACTION STEPS I WILL TAKE TO
ACT LIKE THE PERSON I WANT TO BE

_____

_____

_____

_____

_____

CHAPTER 13

Visualization/Practice

Winners look ahead and see what they want, instead of what they don't want. Use the power of visualization to move toward your goal. A picture is worth a thousand words, and it means the same thing when applied to visualization. The stronger the picture you make, the stronger the results will be. Start to picture the good things you want to happen and you will be a winner as well.

One way to do this is to visualize what you want each night before you go to sleep. Have you noticed when you wake up in the morning, many times you are having the same thoughts you had when you went to sleep? You can use this to your advantage, by making your last thoughts of the day visions of what you want to accomplish, along with positive thoughts about accomplishing it. You will sleep better and move your life ahead as well.

ACTION STEPS I WILL TAKE TO
VISUALIZE WHAT I WANT

_____

_____

_____

_____

_____

If you practice the way you play, there shouldn't be any difference. That is Michael Jordan's secret, and it can be yours as well. Practice as hard as or harder than you play in the game, and the game will seem easy. Also be sure to avoid one of the biggest, and most disastrous, mistakes many people make. That is to change your style once you start to play for real. People say to themselves, "Oh boy, the pressure is really on, so now I am going to change my grip," or something like that, and the results are usually disastrous. Make all your decisions on style, etc., before the pressure is on, and then concentrate on making it happen, once the real thing starts.

ACTION STEPS I WILL TAKE TO
PLAY THE WAY I PRACTICE

_____

_____

_____

_____

_____

CHAPTER 14

Handling Fear and Worry

Many people are afraid of success because they feel that the more they do, the more other people will expect from them. I believe that is true and I also believe that one of the people who should be expecting more is you. Most of us can do more than we are currently doing, and we hold back for various reasons. Whom does this underperformance hurt? In many ways, it's you. If you could do more for your business, isn't there a good chance you would get some reward from it, in some way? The same is true in your personal life. If you could do a better job of watching your diet, or getting more exercise, who would benefit?

I suggest you look at your business or personal life, and pick an area to experiment with. Raise the bar in that area, and do a little more to see what happens. How do you feel about yourself? Did you get any rewards? What did you have to give up to do it? I think you will find that you will give yourself a psychological boost as a result of it, and this boost will cause you to raise the bar again, or to pick another area to experiment in. Don't hold back—give yourself permission to live up to your full potential and you will be surprised at how good you will feel.

ACTION STEPS I WILL TAKE TO INCREASE MY PERFORMANCE

_____

_____

_____

_____

_____

Do your homework in advance, in order to reduce stress in your life. If you want to reduce stress in your life; you need to change before change is necessary. Prevention is cheaper than the cure. If you wait until change is necessary, then you will be under tremendous stress. If you study well in advance of the test, you won't have stress, but if you wait until the night before the test to study, you will be under stress.

So prepare before the big day comes. Look down the road and see what is coming that you can prepare for now. Then take action to do your homework, and be ready when the event you are preparing for comes.

ACTION STEPS I WILL TAKE TO
BE PREPARED IN ADVANCE

_____

_____

_____

_____

CHAPTER 15

Using Your Special Gifts

Use your gifts to the fullest. You probably have several things that you excel at, and you probably don't use those things as often as you should. Time management research consistently shows that people spend most of their time doing things that are not a priority and that do not utilize their special skills to their fullest.

If you do a time log for yourself and track how you spend your time, you will see that those things that you are truly gifted at make up only a small part of your day. Make up a list of two or three things you are really good at and make it a point to spend more time doing things that fall into these skill areas. If you do this, you will see both your productivity and your morale increase. To move your life ahead faster, focus on activities that you are the best at and make a point to spend more and more time just doing those things.

ACTION STEPS I WILL TAKE TO
FOCUS ON USING MY SPECIAL GIFTS

_____

_____

_____

_____

_____

Just like the army advises, be all that you can be. Step back and look at your life, your environment, etc., and ask yourself if you are indeed being all you can be. Imagine if you were an eagle, but somehow you were put into a chicken's nest when you were an egg. You would grow up as a chicken, never using your special skills as an eagle.

Many people are born with special skills, interests, etc., that they never get to use, because they accept their surroundings as a given. They take others' assessments of how they can do in business, or sports, or whatever, and they never live up to their potential.

Take some time off from listening to what others say you can or can't do. Test yourself, push yourself, evaluate yourself and see what you really can do. I believe you will find that you really are an eagle in many ways.

**ACTION STEPS I WILL TAKE TO
FIND OUT HOW GOOD I REALLY AM**

_____

_____

_____

_____

_____

CHAPTER 16

Learn from Failure

Learn from your mistakes. Fail forward. Everyone makes mistakes, but not everyone learns from them. If you had a problem, you have already paid the price, so you might as well learn from it. If you focus on the negative and think of it as a mistake, you will make yourself afraid to move ahead. If you focus on the positive and view it as a learning experience, you will be able to move ahead.

Success really does come from failure, as you learn what doesn't work. Are you making the same mistakes today that you made yesterday? Most of us don't learn from our mistakes, but they are a great source of ways to improve our lives. If you want to move your life ahead faster, look at what you did yesterday and ask yourself these three questions: (1)What didn't I do enough of yesterday, that I can do more of today? (2)What did I do too much of yesterday, that I can do less of today? (3)What new thing can I do today that I didn't do yesterday, that will help me?

ACTION STEPS I WILL TAKE TO
LEARN FROM MY MISTAKES

_____

_____

_____

_____

_____

The secret to success is to keep coming back. Don't take rejection personally. Everyone encounters rejection every day, but not everyone handles it well. Some people quit, some people cut back, but others press on. Be the one who presses on. Most things in life are a numbers game. You have to make x amount of tries before you get what you want. We just don't know what the magic number is, and the only way to find out is to make those tries, until you succeed. Tell yourself, "I am one step closer to making it now."

The only thing you should take personally is the wins. Also remember, every exit is an entrance to somewhere else. When you have obstacles and have a door close on you, another door opens, and it will lead to even better things. Keep opening the doors and success will be yours.

ACTION STEPS I WILL TAKE TO
UTILIZE REJECTION TO HELP ME

_____

_____

_____

_____

_____

CHAPTER 17

Handling Discouragement

You need to develop bounce-back ability. Winners lose more than losers lose, but winners get back up and keep trying until they get it. Losers lose and give up. If you are going to be a winner, you have to keep going, no matter how many times you lose, and sooner or later you will be the winner. Michael Jordan was cut from his high school basketball team in the 10th grade, but he didn't give up. He bounced back, and I don't have to tell you the rest of that story.

You need to focus on the wins that are ahead of you, and not on the losses that are behind you. Learn to bounce back from defeats—this is the difference between winners and losers. Winners all have gone through periods of defeat, but that is all in the past now; the defeats are history, today they are winners. So if you are having defeats, remember that you can quit now and be a loser, but if you keep going, you have a shot at being a winner.

ACTION STEPS I WILL TAKE TO DEVELOP BOUNCE-BACK ABILITY

_____

_____

_____

_____

_____

Don't quit. Many of our failures are caused by our quitting too soon. We get frustrated, angry, tired, etc., and we quit. But much of the time we were almost there and didn't know it. Imagine trying to boil water and then quitting at 211 degrees. That is how it is with many of the things we are involved in. Sure it is hard to keep going, and much of the time we can't see any progress, so here is the time to step back and remind yourself of two things. First remind yourself of what you are trying to accomplish, and more importantly, remind yourself of why you are trying to accomplish it. Once we focus on the why, the problem comes into a different focus and somehow becomes more bearable.

So next time you are having a problem, don't give yourself the option of quitting until you have reviewed why you are doing the action in the first place. If you do that, you will become like Winston Churchill and never, never, never surrender.

ACTION STEPS I WILL TAKE TO
AVOID QUITTING TOO SOON

_____

_____

_____

_____

_____

CHAPTER 18

Going All Out

Can you sing? Can you dance? Can you draw or paint? You probably said "No." Now think back to when you were in kindergarten. What did you say when asked those questions? You said "Yes." Well, what happened since then? You let the magic inside yourself get killed, or drained. Why not start now to get the magic back? Say you can sing, say you can dance and draw, etc. And start doing it. Live life. Don't let other people's opinions, and even worse, your own, kill your life. Live life again.

ACTION STEPS I WILL TAKE TO LIVE LIFE AGAIN

_____

_____

_____

_____

Play to win, not to avoid losing. If your goal is to win, you will take risks and get rewards you wouldn't get if you were just trying to avoid losing. You will play a totally different game. This goes for your whole life, not just a game. Go into your projects with the goal of winning, rather than just to avoid losing.

**ACTION STEPS I WILL TAKE TO
PLAY TO WIN**

_____

_____

_____

_____

_____

CHAPTER 19

Focus

Your focus is your future. You get what you focus on. You can focus on the things that will move you and your projects ahead, or you can focus on things that will not. Focus brings all your power together and enables you to do things in one area that you couldn't do without it. Picture yourself achieving your goals, and your chances of achieving them go up dramatically. Believe it and you will see it.

What you think about on a daily basis is what your future will be like. Tibetan monks believe that if you want to know your future, look at what you are doing right now. Everything we do now affects what will happen next. Our life is a chain of now's and all the things we did in those now's. Now is what counts and now is what will make your future.

ACTION STEPS I WILL TAKE TO
FOCUS ON THINGS THAT WILL HELP ME

_____

_____

_____

_____

_____

Be aware of what can happen to you if you fail, but focus on what you want, and see yourself completing your goal. If I put a plank down on the ground and ask you to walk over it, you could with no problems. But if I put the same plank over an alligator pit, you would fall. That's because you would be looking at the alligators, not the plank. Life is the same way; you will fall if you focus on the problems, so focus instead on what you want.

ACTION STEPS I WILL TAKE TO
FOCUS ON WHAT I WANT

_____

_____

_____

_____

_____

CHAPTER 20

Build on Your Wins

Give yourself credit for your achievements, no matter how small. Keeping track of the things that go right for you builds your self-confidence, and you will find it easier to keep the momentum going in your life and bounce back from setbacks.

Many times, when you are up for a raise or promotion, you are required to go through a review and list your accomplishments. Do the same thing for yourself in your personal life. If you do this, your self-esteem will go up along with your motivation to do more things.

People who succeed concentrate on what they did right, whereas people who fail tend to concentrate on what they did wrong. So after you complete some task or activity, take a moment to tell yourself what you did right, and give yourself credit for it.

**ACTION STEPS I WILL TAKE TO
GIVE MYSELF MORE CREDIT**

_____

_____

_____

_____

_____

Keep moving after you have had a success. Don't lose your momentum—keep going, don't slow down. Things in motion stay in motion, so you won't have to start over if you keep your wins going. Too many of us stop when we have a win, and go back to ground zero. Then we start the long climb back up, taking more time and energy. Find a way to string your wins together, rather than thinking about slacking off after you have had something go your way.

**ACTION STEPS I WILL TAKE TO
KEEP MY MOMENTUM GOING**

_____

_____

_____

_____

_____

CHAPTER 21

Avoid Quitting

Give it your all. Have you heard the expression, "All you can do is all you can do"? That means you should give your all, every bit of your all, to solve your problems. Anything less than your all is not your best effort and not all you can do to solve your problems. If you give it your all, chances are you will solve your problem, but even if you can't you have the satisfaction of knowing you truly tried everything.

**ACTION STEPS I WILL TAKE TO
GIVE IT MY ALL**

_____

_____

_____

_____

_____

Let me make a prediction. Sometime during the day you will become very tired, your energy level will be low, etc. My guess is that this is psychological fatigue, not physical fatigue. What would happen if someone walked up to you while you were feeling that low energy level, and they told you that you had just won $1,000,000? You would be jumping up and down, feeling great. You wouldn't say, "Go away, I'm too tired."

Look at a group of people that just finished playing a basketball game or football game. The winners are jumping up and down and the losers can barely walk off the field, yet they all put out the same energy during the game.

So how do you handle this psychological fatigue? You keep on keeping on. You don't quit; you keep going. In sports, you may have experienced your second wind. The same thing happens with work. If you keep going, your energy comes back. So next time you think you just can't go on, keep on a little bit longer and see if you don't get your second wind on your project.

ACTION STEPS I WILL TAKE TO
OVERCOME PSYCHOLOGICAL FATIGUE

_____

_____

_____

_____

_____

CHAPTER 22

Motivation

Here is the secret to getting more energy. What you need is a BIG project, a REALLY BIG project. It can be a work project, a project around the house, or something like getting in shape, but it must inspire you by being something you really wish would happen. You will have trouble sleeping, you will always be talking about it, reading about it and actually doing it. So find something you really want to happen and move from the planning stage to the doing stage, and you will find that energy you have been looking for.

**ACTION STEPS I WILL TAKE TO
COME UP WITH AN EXCITING PROJECT**

_____

_____

_____

_____

_____

Give yourself a preview of success, and then you will be willing to pay the price of admission. Your motivation to pay the price for success will go up if you give yourself a picture of what it will be like once you attain your goal. Find a way to see the benefits of attaining your goal, before you start on your journey to the top. See how people that are already successful in the field you are striving to succeed in live their lives. See what kind of conditions they work under, see how they work, and see how they play, see who they associate with, etc. That will give you the extra boost of motivation you need to get started and stay on course.

ACTION STEPS I WILL TAKE TO
PREVIEW MY SUCCESS

_____

_____

_____

_____

_____

CHAPTER 23

Struggle

Struggle and difficulty are the keys to getting what you want. Problems teach you to stretch your mental muscles and learn what you need to learn in order to overcome difficulties. Sacrifice winning for improving, for a while.

You need to keep growing. Many of us stop growing mentally about the time we stop growing physically. We stop looking for challenges, we stop taking risks and we stop exploring new things. So make one small change that moves you toward your goal now. Small changes lead to big changes.

Do something every day that you don't want to do. You need to get out of your comfort zone in order to grow. This can be as simple as taking a new route home, or having something different for lunch. Doing new things gives you new knowledge and experiences, and this will ultimately change your behavior in some way. Change your motto to, "If at first you succeed, try something harder," and watch your life take off.

ACTION STEPS I WILL TAKE TO STRETCH MYSELF

_____

_____

_____

_____

_____

Stop running from adversity. Adversity gives us the chance to grow personally and professionally. Here are some of the ways it does this. Adversity brings out our resources by causing us to dig deeper into our pool of skills, in order to solve a problem. Adversity makes life interesting. Believe it or not, life is boring without problems. Adversity brings you closer to other people. You are drawn to co-workers, family, your team, etc.

Adversity builds our character. We need it to grow strong skills in discipline and perseverance. Adversity builds genius, and prosperity conceals it. So remember the words of Napoleon Hill, "Every adversity, every failure, every heartache carries with it the seed of an equal or greater benefit."

ACTION STEPS I WILL TAKE TO EMBRACE ADVERSITY

_____

_____

_____

_____

_____

CHAPTER 24

Take Care of Your Body

If you don't get enough sleep, you won't do as well. Science has proven that your mother was right; there is a link between getting enough sleep and memory and learning ability. If you need to be sharp to learn new things and then remember them, you must get adequate sleep. Make hard choices about what you will do while you are awake, and make a decision to miss doing some things in order to get enough sleep. If your commitment is to do things right and keep learning new things, you must get adequate sleep.

ACTION STEPS I WILL TAKE TO
GET ENOUGH SLEEP

_____

_____

_____

_____

_____

Remember to take care of your body. Your body has to be there for you to make it to the top. Take care of the basics like losing weight, stopping smoking, driving safely, etc. You know what has to be done; the key thing is doing it. It isn't easy, but it is part of the requirements of success.

If your body can't deliver the level of performance the rest of you is capable of, you are robbing yourself of your shot at success. The key isn't finding the perfect system to take care of your body; there are tons of proven systems to get in shape, lose weight, stop smoking, etc. The key is choosing one and sticking to it. They all work, if you work them. Pick a plan and get to work, now.

**ACTION STEPS I WILL TAKE TO
PICK A PLAN AND STICK TO IT**

_____

_____

_____

_____

_____

CHAPTER 25

Bad Habits

Quit it. Stop it right now. You are doing something in your life that is holding back your potential and/or damaging you in some way. It could be physical or mental, but chances are there is something you are doing that you would be better off not doing. Find out what it is, admit it, and find a way to reduce or eliminate it. Your life will move ahead faster and you will probably feel better in the long run, if you stop doing something that is holding you back.

ACTION STEPS I WILL TAKE TO
STOP DOING SOMETHING HARMFUL

_____

_____

_____

_____

_____

Everything counts. When you are working on accomplishing something, you need to realize that everything you do or don't do counts. It is all using your time and energy, taking you towards or away from your goals.

Take yourself and what you do seriously. This doesn't mean you can't have fun and relax, it just means that you can't write sections of your life off. What would you be willing to do if your life depended on it? How your life works depends on what you do with it every minute. Your life depends on how you think, and how you think determines how you act, and how you act determines how your life works.

Think of the things you do as packing your own, as well as others', parachutes. Today's actions will affect you and others to varying degrees in the future. Everything has consequences, good or bad. Focus on the outcomes you want and take actions that will result in consequences that coincide with your goals.

ACTION STEPS I WILL TAKE TO
BE AWARE THAT EVERYTHING COUNTS

_____

_____

_____

_____

CHAPTER 26

Knowledge

Information is the key to success. Information can be gained in many ways; the key thing is to start accumulating it. Read more books, surf the 'net. Every problem you have now and will ever have has been solved by someone else, and they wrote a book about it or posted it on the Internet. The answer to almost every problem you have is as close as your nearest library, book store or computer. If you think the price of a book is high, wait until you see the price of not reading it. Accumulate information on a regular basis—the results will be incredible.

ACTION STEPS I WILL TAKE TO
GAIN MORE INFORMATION

_____

_____

_____

_____

_____

Read 30 minutes of material related to your field each day. Instead of reading you can substitute things like listening to tapes or CDs in your car, or Web browsing, but the key is to spend time every day gaining new knowledge related to your work. The top people in any field get there and stay there by being on the cutting edge of the knowledge in their field. They get this knowledge by reading books, magazines, etc., that cover topics related to their field. Over time people come to realize that the people who keep up with their field are true experts and their reputation builds along with their income. Reading exercises your mind, much like exercise builds your body, and you need both.

ACTION STEPS I WILL TAKE TO
READ MATERIAL RELATED TO MY FIELD

_____

_____

_____

_____

_____

CHAPTER 27

Improving

What would you be doing right now, if you knew you were really going to get what you wanted? If you knew you were going to get what you wanted, you would probably be concentrating more on the skills needed to get the thing you want. You also would realize that once you made it, you would have to perform at a certain level, but you would realize you aren't ready now. Therefore, you would begin to put a greater effort into getting ready.

Well, why not get ready anyway, even if you don't know whether you are going to make it? This will help insure that you will get what you want, since once you have the skills and interest, there isn't much more you will need, except to keep looking for the right opportunity.

ACTION STEPS I WILL TAKE TO
GET READY FOR MY BIG BREAK

_____

_____

_____

_____

82

Do you want to get better at something? Here is a technique to make you better at it in seven days. Every day ask yourself these four questions regarding the area you want to be better at: (1) What did I do today that I must stop doing, in order to improve? (2) What didn't I do today that I must start doing, in order to improve? (3) What did I do today that I should continue doing, in order to get better? (4) Did I take action on each of these questions?

Pick one thing you want to get better at, and do this exercise for the next seven days. The result will be real improvement.

ACTION STEPS I WILL TAKE TO
GET BETTER AT SOMETHING

_____

_____

_____

_____

_____

CHAPTER 28

Long-Term Satisfaction

Focus on long-term satisfaction, not satisfaction right now. Many times what we want right now will work against what we want long term, and we need to let the long-term goal overrule the short-term goal. For instance, our long-term goal might be to lose weight, but we want a candy bar now. If we choose the candy bar, we are working against the long-term goal of losing weight. Even if we end up choosing the short-term goal, at least we became aware that we have a longer-term goal we are in conflict with, and over time we may begin to choose the longer-term goal on a more consistent basis.

Constantly review where you are heading long term and compare that to what you want at this moment. The choice you make right now can move you closer to your long-term goal, or away from it.

ACTION STEPS I WILL TAKE TO
FOCUS ON MY LONG-TERM GOALS

_____

_____

_____

_____

_____

Many times you have to do what you have to do, before you get to do what you want to do. Most people have to be a student before they are a teacher, or an employee before they are the boss. A commitment to a long-range goal can be the secret to getting through all those things you don't want to do, but have to do.

If you are in a small business and doing many, many different things, such as sweeping the floors and doing errands, etc., chances are you aren't too thrilled about some of these things. And it is easy to get demoralized over this, since these types of jobs always seem to take more time than the stuff you had in mind when you opened the business.

I urge you to find some method of stepping back from the "grunt" work and reminding yourself of your ultimate goal in all of this. See yourself doing what your ultimate objective is. Once you do that, you will be able to go back to the things you have to do, secure in the knowledge that you are on your way to doing what you want to do.

**ACTION STEPS I WILL TAKE TO
REMIND MYSELF OF MY ULTIMATE GOAL**

_____

_____

_____

_____

CHAPTER 29

Handling Irritations

Having trouble with the expression, "There is always a little good, in every bad"? No one wants problems; however, there are generally some good things hidden in with the bad things that are causing your problems.

Here is how you find the good things. Take your biggest problem and then start making a list of all the good things or opportunities this problem brings. Be outrageous, think outside the box, think positive, and keep pushing yourself to come up with more and more ways the bad thing could help you, no matter how silly they sound. Once you have a long list, study it, and you will be amazed to find that there are in fact some good things that came as a result of your problem. The next thing to do is make sure you take advantage of those good things you paid such a price to get.

ACTION STEPS I WILL TAKE TO
FIND THE GOOD AMONG THE BAD

_____

_____

_____

_____

_____

Make a list of all the things you are tolerating in your life, no matter how big or small. You probably have a long list of things you are putting up with, because you don't want to spend the time and/or money to fix them. They range from a burned-out light bulb to a car that needs repair. You probably are not aware that each of these things drains energy from you at some level. Every time you have to deal with it, it causes frustration, anger, etc., as well as a loss of efficiency in some area of your life.

Take steps to begin to rid yourself of the smaller things and watch your energy level begin to rise. You will build the resolve to tackle larger and larger things in your life that are problems for you. Start that list of aggravations now, then start fixing them, and watch your mood improve along with your accomplishments.

ACTION STEPS I WILL TAKE TO ELIMINATE AGGRAVATIONS

_____

_____

_____

_____

_____

CHAPTER 30

Work Smarter

Don't work harder, work smarter. What can you do on your job, right now, to work smarter? What you did yesterday to be smarter doesn't count. Things have changed since then and you have to relook at things every day. You have new information, perhaps new tools, and new challenges and opportunities, so look around you right now and see what you can do better, faster, cheaper, and, of course, smarter.

**ACTION STEPS I WILL TAKE TO
WORK SMARTER TODAY**

_____

_____

_____

_____

_____

Take care of the basics, as well as the big picture. Most battles are not won; they are lost. Most of the victories we see occur because the other side did something to lose; they made some mistakes that cost them the battle. So look at how you can make sure you don't do anything to cause you to lose your battle, as well as looking at what you can do to win the battle. Get your act together, cover the basics and be prepared to do everything right before you embark on your project.

ACTION STEPS I WILL TAKE TO
COVER THE BASICS

_____

_____

_____

_____

_____

CHAPTER 31

Positive Attitude

Be your own fortune-teller and predict good things for yourself. Here is a trick that fortune-tellers use to predict someone's future that you can use on yourself. Fortune-tellers quickly get a sense of what a person is thinking—are they positive, negative, etc. Then they can project what will happen, given that type of thinking. You can do this with yourself. If you are positive, good things are going to happen to you; if you are pessimistic, things are going to go badly for you.

If you want to predict a good future for yourself, act positive, think positive, etc., and the world will be yours. Always be positive about yourself when you talk. If you're negative, it causes others to lose faith in you, and you also lose faith in yourself. Always be positive in your speech, regardless of whether someone else is around, as you are the most important person that will hear it.

Remember, your attitude is contagious to others as well as to yourself, so predict good fortune for yourself and others and it will come true.

ACTION STEPS I WILL TAKE TO
PREDICT GOOD THINGS FOR MYSELF

_____

_____

_____

_____

_____

Right now, look into yourself and find one self-limiting belief you have and toss it out. Every one of us carries around many beliefs that we take for granted, that hold us back. We hold them inside us, unchallenged, and they work silently to hold us back when we try to move ahead. Most of these ideas won't stand up to the light of day if challenged. In addition, most were formed long ago, and you are a different person now, with new skills, etc. So, right now, look into some of your beliefs about yourself and find one that is just not true, and discard it.

ACTION STEPS I WILL TAKE TO
ELIMINATE SELF-LIMITING BELIEFS

_____

_____

_____

_____

_____

CHAPTER 32

Change

Let the hurt in, if you want to change. Psychologists agree that when the hurt is big enough, the will to change emerges. So let the hurt in, rather than hiding it, and it will give you the momentum to change.

One other thing that will help you to change, particularly if you are trying to change a habit, is to replace the old habit with a brand new habit. This will fill the void you feel from the loss of the old habit.

Lastly, once you have begun to change, stop playing victim and give yourself credit for being a new person. Being a victim robs you of your sense of self-control and undercuts your ability to make changes.

ACTION STEPS I WILL TAKE TO
LET THE HURT IN

_____

_____

_____

_____

Spring or not, it is time for some spring-cleaning of your values. Time has passed, you have grown and changed, yet you probably have kept many of the same values, ideas, etc., that you always had. Take some time to think about what really matters to you and write it down. Then ask yourself if you are acting on these items in terms of what you are doing on a day-to-day basis.

If you are like most people, you will discover that you value things differently than you used to and that you haven't adjusted how you live your life to the new values. While you are doing this spring-cleaning of your mind, take a look at other things that are outmoded. Perhaps you associate with people who no longer share your values. These people can drain you if they are negative and are pulling you down.

Start to gradually phase in new actions that reflect how you view things today, and phase out activities that do not correspond to your new values. You will feel new energy and satisfaction with life and find you are more successful in what you do. Set up a schedule to review your goals and objectives and see how you are doing versus your target. This will help you keep your life on track and let you take corrective action as needed.

ACTION STEPS I WILL TAKE TO
UPDATE MY VALUES

_____

_____

_____

_____

_____

CHAPTER 33

Feedback

Maybe your critics are right and maybe they are wrong. Either way, it pays to listen to them. Listen to the negative things people say about you, and as much as it hurts, think about it and see if there is any validity to it. If so, your critics did you a favor. That is some feedback that tells you an area to work on which you may not be addressing, and the world is telling you it is time to pay attention. Give some thought to what they say and what you can do to get better in that area.

On the other hand, don't be too fast to accept criticism or rejection. Feedback is useful, but the critics can be wrong. When you are rejected or criticized, step back and consider keeping going, rather than giving up or changing. History is full of examples of ideas that were rejected, which then went on to change the world. So don't give up on your ideas, unless you are convinced that they won't work.

**ACTION STEPS I WILL TAKE TO
CONSIDER CRITICISM GIVEN ME**

_____

_____

_____

_____

_____

You need feedback to know when you are off course. Spacecraft that go to the moon make millions of corrections on the flight based on feedback that they are off course, and eventually they make it. The same should be true for you. Constantly look for feedback as to how you are doing, and then make the adjustments you need to stay on course.

Listen to the people around you. People can give you feedback about many of the things we tend to be oblivious to. Sometimes others see things about us that we would prefer not to see, but which we need to know about. Other times they see things a different way, because their value systems are different, but they can give us an idea we wouldn't have thought about. So listen to other people, especially the people you trust, and pay attention to what they say. You may come away with new insights.

ACTION STEPS I WILL TAKE TO LISTEN TO FEEDBACK

_____

_____

_____

_____

_____

CHAPTER 34

Problems

Problems can be the big break you have been looking for. Be a problem seeker, not just a problem solver. Solving problems is great, but the real opportunity for success lies in seeking out problems, and then solving them.

Most successful new businesses are built on taking problems and solving them in a way that people will pay for. Every problem you encounter is your opportunity if you can be the one to solve it. Looking at problems as opportunities helps you move through them faster and easier, even if you don't turn them into a new business.

Rather than avoiding problems, or fretting about problems, you should spend time looking into the problems, their causes and, of course, the fixes. You will feel good about doing it, and it will help move your life ahead.

**ACTION STEPS I WILL TAKE TO
LOOK AT PROBLEMS AS OPPORTUNITIES**

_____

_____

_____

_____

_____

Solve the problem, rather than be right. Many of us focus on being right, rather than solving the problem. The time we spend defending our position, attacking others, etc., takes away from getting the job done. Leave your ego out of it, and focus on getting the job done.

Needing to be right causes us and our projects to get stuck. Get unstuck and new things in you and others will emerge, plus you will accomplish your goal. Admit your mistakes and move on. Tying up your time and energy with mistakes holds you back in many ways, and it hurts your relations with other people.

Also, stop punishing yourself for mistakes. Many people go through life with a "record" of their past mistakes, and this condemns them to a future much like the past. Don't dwell on the mistakes by repeatedly bringing them up. Acknowledge your mistake, fix it, lighten up on yourself and move forward.

ACTION STEPS I WILL TAKE TO
MAKE SOLVING THE PROBLEM MY FOCUS

CHAPTER 35

Getting on with Life

Play the cards you have been dealt. Don't try to change what you have been given up to this point; focus on using what you have now, where you are now, right now. You can change your future, but you can't change your past. You can learn from your past, but you must take what you have and make the best of it from this point on. Don't waste time complaining about the bad hand life has given to you. Life is not always about liking what you have; sometimes it is about doing the best you can with what you have and getting on with it.

You have to ask yourself what you can change and what is going to stay with you, no matter what. Then work on the things you can change, and get your satisfaction from being in the process of change, rather than focusing on the conditions you are in at the moment. Make the best of your hand and move on to the next hand or even a new game, but use what you have as the base.

ACTION STEPS I WILL TAKE TO
PLAY THE CARDS I HAVE BEEN DEALT

_____

_____

_____

_____

_____

It's a good thing you didn't get what you wanted. In this world, everything really does happen for the best, and what happened, even if it was not what you wanted, is the best thing that could have happened to you. When one door closes for you, another door opens. It is up to you to find that other door, open it and find out why it was the best thing for you. Work at finding the good among the bad, picking up the pieces and going on with your life, by taking the setback and turning it into something positive.

ACTION STEPS I WILL TAKE TO
VIEW WHAT HAPPENS AS THE BEST

_____

_____

_____

_____

_____

CHAPTER 36

Flexibility

Football players learn that despite the blocking and tackling, the ball is never where it is supposed to be, and they must adapt to the situation as it exists at the moment. Army Rangers have this saying: "Once the first shot is fired, all the plans are out the window."

Things are constantly changing, and no matter how well we plan, things are going to turn up that we didn't plan on. This doesn't mean we shouldn't plan, but it does mean we have to be flexible and open to change. Look at how you handle changes to the situation your plans are based on. Ask yourself if you need to be more adaptable and if you need to build more contingency plans into your thought process.

ACTION STEPS I WILL TAKE TO
BE READY TO CHANGE COURSE

_____

_____

_____

_____

_____

Increase your options. Develop a second, or even a third set of skills to fall back on, in case your current job or trade is lost or reduced in importance. Don't focus too much on one occupation; rather, develop a range of skills that can be used in case your main occupation is lost. A person with a range of skills worries less about things being out of control, economic downturns, etc. You don't feel locked into one occupation or career and you are flexible enough to take advantage of other opportunities as they come along.

Begin to take steps to build a "fall-back" occupation or career by taking night classes, starting a part-time business, or doing other things to gain knowledge and experience in another field. That way you will have the peace of mind that comes with the knowledge that your world doesn't hinge on one particular job or career path.

ACTION STEPS I WILL TAKE TO
BUILD A BACK-UP OCCUPATION

_____

_____

_____

_____

_____

CHAPTER 37

Pay Attention

Invest your time instead of spending your time. If you are doing something, put your all into it. If you are practicing something, concentrate on doing it right; don't just go through the motions. Pay attention to what you are doing and concentrate on accomplishing something as a result of your effort and time. You are paying the price in terms of time—you might as well get the most you can out of it, and you will move your life ahead faster.

You can't control the outcome of things, but you can control the effort that goes into the preparation. And you have control of your attitude, so if you give your best efforts and keep up your best attitude, chances are very good you will get the outcome you desire.

Remember that the will to win is not as important as the will to prepare to win. Everyone wants to win, but not everyone wants to prepare to win. Preparing to win is where the determination that you will win is made. Once the game, or test, or project is underway, it is too late to prepare to win. The actual game, test, or project is the end of a long process of getting ready, in which the outcome was determined in the preparation stage. So if you want to win, you must prepare to win.

ACTION STEPS I WILL TAKE TO PREPARE TO WIN

_____

_____

_____

_____

_____

The secret of doing anything better is to pay attention to it when you are doing it. The quality of work that comes out of a job is in direct proportion to the amount of attention given to the job. You can't do two things at once, at least not well, so focus on what you are doing, and the job will turn out better.

Stop multitasking and start maxi accomplishing. Treat each task you do as if it is the most important thing you have to do, because if you are using time management skills correctly, it will be. Poorly executed tasks have a way of coming back to you. They undercut other people's confidence in you and they undercut your own self-confidence and pride.

ACTION STEPS I WILL TAKE TO
PAY MORE ATTENTION TO THINGS

_____

_____

_____

_____

_____

CHAPTER 38

Procrastination

Act as if. That's right, act as if. Whatever you want, act as if you already have it. If you are in a bad mood, act as if you are in a good mood. Go around smiling, hold your head high, sing, and walk proud. Within minutes, you will find yourself in a good mood. Facing a chore you don't want to do? Act as if you want to do it and start doing it. Within a few minutes, you will be enjoying it.

On a longer-term basis, if you want to achieve a goal, act as if you have already achieved it and guess what? You will achieve it. That is the key to getting what you want. Act as if you already have it and it will be yours.

**ACTION STEPS I WILL TAKE TO
ACT AS IF**

_____

_____

_____

_____

_____

Give me 15 minutes and I'll put you on your way to completing your project. If you are working on something you don't want to work on, and are about to quit, here is a tip for you. Work on it for 15 minutes, and I mean really work on it, rather than just going through the motions. Guess what? After 15 minutes you will find yourself interested in what you are doing, you will really be into it, and most of the time you will find it hard to quit. If you set out to work on it at least 15 minutes, chances are you will find yourself finishing the project.

**ACTION STEPS I WILL TAKE TO
WORK AT LEAST 15 MINUTES ON A TASK**

CHAPTER 39

Balance/Fun

You probably need more balance in your life, regarding your basic issues. Ask yourself these age-old questions. Do you view wealth as having the most, or is wealth needing the least? Are you giving up your health to accumulate wealth, just to lose your weath to try to regain your health? Are you worrying so much about the future that you have no present? Are you living as though you will never die, and setting yourself up to die as though you never lived?

The answer to these questions is balance. Everything we do as well as don't do in life has a price. Step back now and look to see if you need more balance in your life, and start now to regain it. It has been said that every man dies, but not every man lives. You need balance in your life if you work too hard, or play too hard, at the expense of the other parts of your life. You can't neglect your health, or your personal life for your professional life, for too long, without paying the price. All the parts of your life contribute to your total success, and you need each part to make it to the top and stay there.

**ACTION STEPS I WILL TAKE TO
ACHIEVE MORE BALANCE IN MY LIFE**

_____

_____

_____

_____

_____

Goals are nice, but don't forget to live your life. When we have goals, we sometimes stop thinking about the present, and the present is where we live. Find something to be happy for *now*.

There is always something that we are waiting for and then life will begin. Stop waiting until you get that promotion, raise, perfect mate, etc., so you can be happy. It is nice to attain the big goals, but usually the glow of achievement is short-lived and we need to move on to the next goal. There will always be problems in your life and there will always be things that you want. If you wait for your problems to go away, or until you have the perfect life, you will never be happy.

You must choose to be happy independently of events that life throws you, or if you haven't achieved your goal yet. Learn to be happy as you are in the process of attaining your goals, or learn to be happy with what you have now, where you are for the moment. Get on with your life and start smiling.

ACTION STEPS I WILL TAKE TO BE HAPPY NOW

_____

_____

_____

_____

_____

CHAPTER 40

Comfort Zone

Are you stuck in your comfort zone? Most of us get stuck in our comfort zone, and while we realize that in order to make progress we need to be uncomfortable, such as experiencing rejections, setbacks, etc., we are not able to break out of it. Here are four things you can do right now to get out of your comfort zone: (1) Recognize that you are in a comfort zone by recognizing that you have become used to things as they are. (2) Recommit to your goals and bring back your motivation to forge ahead, no matter what. (3) Think about what will happen if you stay in your comfort zone; usually you will not like what you see. (4) Start taking action right now to get yourself out of your comfort zone and into the success zone.

The only way you are going to make progress is to be uncomfortable. You need to get comfortable with being uncomfortable. Any time you are learning something new, stretching yourself, or doing something extra, it is going to feel uncomfortable, tiring or even painful. This is a sign you pushed yourself and you can take this as an award or recognition of your efforts. So take the pain as a positive and go on for more of it, in order to make progress.

ACTION STEPS I WILL TAKE TO MOVE OUT OF MY COMFORT ZONE

_____

_____

_____

_____

_____

You must reinvent yourself every several years. Given the current rate of change in the world, very little of what we know or do will be relevant five years from now. If we are going to continue to offer value to the world and to ourselves, we must make changes to insure we are in sync with what the world wants and needs.

Companies are constantly offering "new and improved" versions of their products, and we must do likewise. Those of us on the top now must change to remain on top, and those wanting to move up can use this need to change as a new opportunity to grow and gain.

Reinventing ourselves is hard work and takes lots of research and soul-searching, but the payoff is renewed vigor and strength, improved morale, a greater sense of self-satisfaction, and financial rewards. So start taking an inventory of what you have to offer, versus what the world is going to want. Begin to do things such as taking classes, gaining practical experience, etc., in areas you see as necessary for your growth.

ACTION STEPS I WILL TAKE TO
REINVENT MYSELF

_____

_____

_____

_____

_____

CHAPTER 41

Increase Your Sense of Control

If you want to increase your sense of control, you need to give yourself more areas in your life where you make choices. Every day you make choices about your behavior, your attitude and your decisions. These choices come from either your habits or your thinking. These both come from within you and they are the only things in life you can control.

We all tend to think we are in control until things go wrong, and then we lose our sense of control. The way to get it back is to return to our options for choices and see where we can expand them. Adding options for choices adds to our being in control.

ACTION STEPS I WILL TAKE TO
INCREASE THE CHOICES I MAKE

_____

_____

_____

_____

_____

It is not the circumstances; it is you. Everything bad that happens to us can be blamed on the circumstances. If you want something good to happen to you, take something bad that happened to you, and blame yourself. Once you take responsibility for a problem, even if it wasn't your fault, things will start to go better for you. You will look at what you can learn from a problem, and you will feel more in control. No excuses, no matter what happens. Don't make excuses to anyone, especially yourself. Take full responsibility for what went wrong, whether it was your fault or not. This will lead people to respect you more, and your self-respect will increase as well.

Once you know you are going to be taking responsibility for everything, you will perform everything you do at a higher level, to make sure it comes out well. There will be fewer things to make excuses for. People will give you more and more responsibility and trust, thus moving your life ahead. So no excuses, just results—and good things will come to you.

ACTION STEPS I WILL TAKE TO
ASSUME RESPONSIBILITY FOR A PROBLEM

_____

_____

_____

_____

_____

CHAPTER 42

Let Your Ideas Out

Be one of the crazy ones. Don't be afraid to be outrageous. Don't be afraid of the word "no." Some of the greatest people in the world were considered outrageous in their time and they heard plenty of "no's," but they kept on, and today the world is theirs.

There is no need for more of what we already have. We need something different and you can be the one to give it to us. The greatest people that have ever lived, the people that have made breakthroughs, have all had characteristics that would make them seem crazy.

Thinking that you can change the world just might make it possible that you *can* change the world in some way. Others may think you are crazy, but it is the genius inside you that is giving you those thoughts. Let your crazy thoughts come and success will follow.

ACTION STEPS I WILL TAKE TO
KEEP PUSHING MY IDEAS

_____

_____

_____

_____

_____

127

You are a salesperson, whether you know it or not. You are always selling your ideas to others, even if they are not "customers" in the classic sense. So if you want to improve your rate of "sales," or be more convincing to others, change your attitude to viewing yourself as *helping* others, instead of selling others.

You have great ideas, products, etc., so you are in fact helping other people if they use them. If you had the latest invention in the fight to cure a disease, you wouldn't be bashful about asking people to use it would you? Think of yourself the same way with whatever idea or product you are trying to get across and you will become "Salesperson of the Year."

**ACTION STEPS I WILL TAKE TO
VIEW MYSELF AS HELPING OTHERS**

_____

_____

_____

_____

_____

CONCLUSION

Sixty Seconds to Success was intended to give you quick, action-oriented steps to take, which will move your life ahead even faster. I hope you will use this book on a regular basis and implement at least one of the tips each day. One thing is clear: nothing will happen without action on your part. *Sixty Seconds to Success* has given you the tools, now it is up to you to use them. If you do, I know your whole life will be a Bright Moment.

I would like to leave you with a quote from the unknown author who wrote my favorite bumper sticker:

"Life is a gift, that's why they call it the present."

Submit Your Own Ideas

Here is your chance to contribute to the next edition of *Sixty Seconds to Success.* If you have a suggestion for a tip on moving one's life forward even faster, which can be used in the next edition of *Sixty Seconds to Success*, please send it to me. If it is used, you will receive an autographed copy of the next edition prior to it being sold to the public, and you will receive credit in the book. Also, if you have any suggestions or comments on *Sixty Seconds to Success*, we would like to receive those as well. Please send suggestions, comments, etc., to:

Bright Moment
P. O. Box 8106
Englewood, NJ 07631-8106
or e-mail to edsmith@brightmoment.com.

ORDER FORM

Internet Orders: Order online at Brightmoment.com.

Mail Orders: Bright Moment, Post Office Box 8106
                     Englewood, NJ 07631-8106. 201-568-0019

Shipping Address: (please print)

Name _____

Street Address _____ Apt. _____

City _____ State _____ Zip _____

Country _____

Phone Number including area code _____

E-mail _____

Quantity ordered _____ @ $13.95 Subtotal $ _____

Sales Tax   NJ residents add 6%   Tax $ _____

Shipping and handling
    at $3.95 each (USA only) $ _____

Shipping and handling
    at $10 each (non-USA orders) $ _____

                            Total $ _____

Payment Method:

Check (Payable to Bright Moment in US funds only) _____

Credit Card: Visa_____ MasterCard_____

Card Number _____

Exp. date _____

Name on Credit Card _____

Cardholder Signature _____